On Ruben Slikk
A Manifesto on the Purpose of Art and the Value of Transgression

Caleb True

On Ruben Slikk

Capitol Hill, D.C., Echo Park, Los Angeles, Seattle, and St. Louis

Cover design by David Croy.

Printed in the U.S.A.

10   9   8   7   6   5   4   3   2   1   blast off.

Dynamoverlag.com

DYNAMO
VERLAG

ECLECTICISM | GENIUS | ORIGINALITY

Table Of Contents

Introduction

Rap comes from a dissenting place, but these days it is also front and center in the pop music world. Now, pop music is mostly a remixing of clichés from which to build a sonic something just original enough that litigation can be avoided while money is being made. It's mammonistic and aurally addictive—whether we desire it, pop choruses linger on in our heads. Stream-lined, slick, characterized by vocal swoops into falsetto register cathartically illustrating easily digestible apho-risms about reality. Beyond its component parts and its economic purpose, pop music is difficult to describe in a way that doesn't come off as advertorial. If I have a gripe with mainstream music criticism, it is for the same reason: it feels mainly commercial, an auxiliary to industry sales and little else. Engines for pop music criticism, even the best of them, dress up contemporary pop in exquisite prose, and suggest that it might have something to offer a well-educated mind over and above the obvious; something beyond the commercial; something to appreciate the way a connoisseur might. Pop criticism makes pop music consumers feel good about having banal tastes—and it makes *all* consumers lazy about looking for music that might actually be worth listening to.

I first encountered Ruben Slikk's music on a friend's phone, sitting in the backseat of a car on the way to a literary festival in Virginia. The person who showed me Slikk on his phone was a graduate school colleague of mine. It was not specifically a Ruben Slikk track that he played for us, but rather one of his musical groups, Metro Zu, a trio which includes his brother and a third member. My friend must have thought the song was very funny, or very outrageous, or both. I think the song found my friend by word of mouth through his Florida connections, as Slikk comes from the rich milieu of south Florida soundcloud rap—a particularly extreme strain of a subset of rap that is already known for being wilder, or more extreme (and often looser) than its more mainstream parent, and from the US state already famous, among states, for its extremes.

Oddballs like Ruben Slikk, I think, must be happened upon by accident. Slikk's music *sounds* enough like pop music, even if it is a bit rough around the edges. But then, there are little things that creep in. The sardonic timbre of Slikk's voice, almost from the first utterance. And then there are the lyrics. If most popular music these days is an exercise in *not* calling attention to itself, so as to hide perfectly in playlists with its similars, lyrics in a Slikk song tend to stand out. Vulgarity isn't quite the aim; shock might be. Profanity used to be, in and of itself, a means by which to shock, but these days so much has become acceptable. Pop music has a great deal of profanity, so profanity alone no longer is notable or interesting. But let's bring the word vulgar back for a second. Is Slikk's music vulgar tonally, lyrically? Is his message somehow more vulgar because his word choice is more direct, because it often lacks the *de rigeur* filter of careful metaphor common to other pop artists who are essentially cracking the same lascivious little jokes? Perhaps 'crude' is a better term, but I am troubled by how both of these terms can also simply mean 'underrealized,' or 'colloquial,' or 'primitive,' thus do such terms delegitimize the dismissal of his work altogether.

I would posit that Ruben Slikk actually has quite a lot in common with some bygone jaded love crooners—Ray Price, for instance. Slikk may take a tactile, anatomical, physiological approach to the exploration of one side of what one might call love, but the attitude is the same. Price is a ruthless heaper of blame, a self-absolver, a self-congratulator. He has a gift for double-speak. In short, he is a monster, a real Ted Hughes type, a cannibal in love. But in Price, there's a striving for irreality similar to that in Ruben Slikk's self-mythologizing. Price, too, works in a jive-talking mode, even if he lacks some of the verve and swerve of the real thing. For better and worse, Price self-mythologizes as a kind of *gangsta*, a kind of *pimp*. For better *and* worse. Slikk, for his part, works in a similar vein; his is a self-obsessed, self-beloved, rakish bardism. I don't see his similars among his Spotify genre stamps, those algorithmic keywords which shunt an artist into a box with some others. Rather, Slikk's playful if relentless shockery is more akin to Goethe's *Venetian Epigrams*, Catullus' dirty Latin poems, George Bataille's erotic fiction, Pasolini's most antifascist work, and perhaps the more needling of Frank Zappa's libretti. Which is to say Slikk is working in a transgressive mode; politically, socially, perhaps even linguistically. He is more than just another recording artist with crass lyrics intent on shocking and eliciting prurient giggles. His Proustian output attests to something greater; some consistent, larger purpose. More than his music, his entire public persona forwards a singular vision of mad libertinism and swaggering disregard for authority. His afrofuturist aesthetic alloys to his roving, satirical explorations of sex, drugs, gangsterism, and—yes, indeed—religion to create something uniquely monolithic, vast, disturbing, and, all the time, guilt-inducingly funny. There are plenty of reasons to deliberate.

Creation Anxiety, Cultural Anarchism,[1] Talent, and Merit

Our current era is defined much more by curation than by creation, and there are a couple reasons for this. Macrocuration by algorithm, in music most visibly by Spotify, but also, past and present, by many other competitors, has made many creatives painfully aware of the sheer volume of artistic production in the world. Much human output can be consumed free, or free-with-a-catch, through subscription services that trade one's personal information and/or token payment for incomprehensibly vast volumes of consumable units of

---

[1]Since I don't explicitly define this term in the course of my argument, *cultural anarchism* is the position that all cultural institutions, given enough time, degrade art—the most deleterious among them being those that are commercially oriented, those which owe their very existence to the drawing of profit from art and artworks.

art. This leaves plenty of room for anxiety. The individual artist cannot escape a sense of atomization in such a world, a world in which she is of mindboggling insignificance, attempting to compete with a million other artists like herself, for the viewing, reading, or listening minutes of the masses.

Of course, the trend to curation (and away from creation)—which owes much to internet platforms that equalize those who create content with those who simply pick and choose their favorites from among others' content—has been scaled horizontally, such that we now have millions of *curators* collected under the umbrella of single platforms, curators who knowingly or unknowingly make those platforms money, and who, in turn, harvest their material from further millions of *creators* of content. Thus does genre become more important than the individual artist's style, message, or any true sense of originality or inimitability. The better an individual creator (we might as well stop pretending that every musicmaker is an artist) can match or slot into certain genres, the more likely they will find, by channels, an audience, and, consequently, those precious minutes of strangers' time which can then be translated, if one is very lucky, into some kind of career and some kind of remuneration, either through live performances, invitation to perform at festivals, or through direct sales of music through an obsolete medium such as vinyl, cassette, or CD—a process much more difficult for a macrocurator like Spotify to disrupt. This kind of artistic-living trajectory, which is easy enough to envision and even seems achievable, is in fact so difficult to actualize, and so rare, that unless an artist devotes himself, from a very young age, to achieving not *artistic* actualization, but financial actualization *through* art—through an early self-subjugation to genre markers and keywords that determine an artist's 'discoverability'—it is extremely unlikely that he will ever be able to make a career out of art. To put it another way, without an early surrender to the grand, overlapping systems of curation which run—and run through—social media, he will never be able to draw in-kind compensation for the hours put into his art. To succeed as a recording artist is to win the lottery, in every respect.

So, the upshot? There are a few responses to the horrible prospects for an artist. One can ignore the systems entirely, and profess and enact a technologically-isolated praxis. This is, or was, one punk rock trajectory—the Do It Yourself ethos, vertical and horizontal integration of all parts of the creative process, from scribbling lyrics in a notebook to burning CDs and xeroxing artwork, booking and playing shows, and selling one's handwrought work. For distribution there was a proliferation, in the three eras of punk rock—'77-'83, '88-'93, and '97-'06, approximately—of 'distros,' or little boxes of different groups' merchandise, carried neutrally by roadies and bands on tour, to have something to sell besides one's own merchandise. In addition to being an efficient means of expanding the likelihood of drawing gas/food/lodging money out of a crowd of like-minded strangers, it also drastically expanded the 'discoverability' in a pre-internet age of all those who happened to be included in a given distro box. One went to a show, wandered over to the merch table, and rifled through the distro box. It was a wonderfully simple means of putting one's art in front of strangers. Those bands who had wonderful, outrageous, or clever artwork had an edge over those who didn't, and might have been more likely to be picked up—'discovered'—by someone with an open mind who wandered by. It was hand-selling, but in an expanded, collective way. Two bands, friendly with one another, could carry each others' music on their respective tours, potentially doubling their exposure. Those two bands in turn could swap distro box merch with two others, and suddenly the potential exposure has increased exponentially. It's obvious marketing, but it's also marketing without the unclean residue, the *slime* of marketing. This method worked wonderfully for many. Of course, it relies on a healthy musical subculture in many cities and towns, a 'scene' that a band or artist can tap into favorably while on tour—expecting part or all of a local 'scene' to show up to a show, say; expecting that word-of-mouth networks will effectively make those in a local scene aware of said show, and on and on. It was an enterprise built on mutual interest and good-faith, and correspondingly fragile.

At times when a healthy punk—or otherwise well-integrated DIY—subculture exists, these tactics for building an artistic community might be some of the best, and some of the most fulfilling around, as they eschew alienating technologies in favor of socializing. Everything is person-to-person, everything handmade. Even the music of punk is, or was, anti-virtual, with little or no reliance on synthesizers or non-human-generated sound. But I'm getting ahead of myself: the method of abstention from the systems of macrocuration works only when the appropriate subcultures exist. Usually, these require unified movements among youth, so good luck getting it done if you're over twenty.

The second method for navigating an artistic life might be to selectively address certain platforms, to attempt to master one or two of them as an efficient use of time and energy, at the expense of all the others. This may have been easier in the past, when there were more platforms sharing the market, and the environment for social media was generally more tentative, with all parties feeling their way towards some kind of corporate monopoly, and no clear victor. Now, there seems only to be Spotify and those who are branding against Spotify—e.g. soundcloud, bandcamp. Still, one might successfully maximize their exposure through one of these platforms without really benefitting. An in-person, old-fashioned musical community might still allow for the most useful expansion of a virtual network, but still it will have but a slim fraction of the potential reach of someone who has mastered the platform. Far beyond Spotify, the use of hybrid platforms, those which are both musical and visual—Instragram, Snapchat, TikTok, and so on—might quickly surmount

Spotify as the most important platforms for artistic reach. Which is sad for many, because they seem to benefit a certain socioeconomic stratum (no surprises there), a certain standard of attractiveness, and a certain utter basicness of character. To master TikTok one must be decidedly average in the most heightened, privileged way. Suddenly, a musician, or musical artist, might find herself competing with creators of 'content,' that nebulous catch-all, for attention. Since 'content' on platforms like Instagram and TikTok tends to be addictive-impulse–driven, any kind of art which fails to fire the addiction center of the brain (that isn't catchy, or titillating, or anxiety- or rage-inducing) will lose out. People will swipe away, to the next... to the next...

Perhaps less dire, but no less concerning, that same musical artist who manages to be in some way unique or original—who might, dare I say, be a genius—might be lost amid the miasma of average technical talent: the easiest kind of talent to applaud or ratify, that which can be universally praised with little thought or consideration, and which is often enough, sadly enough, endorsed and elevated by supposedly high-culture engines—magazines or journals or online publications—which have attained clout over the years and always benefit from championing agreeable, easily-digested talent.

While there is as-yet no obvious line from TikTok to mainstream recording contract,[2] it must be just a matter of time before social media platforms like it become *the* field from which the next generation of superstars are harvested. It is indeed a meritocracy, but one absolutely *glutted* with merit—those 'deserving of praise or reward'—and little else. No definition of merit that I have found mentions genius or originality, but 'virtue' and 'entitlement' come up a lot, and there will always be a hundred thousand entitled souls for every genius. Additionally, true genius tends to lack entitlement, and to have little time for virtue, and both entitlement and virtue have far more to do with publicity and promo-

---

[2]I'm sure less obvious ones exist.

tion than with anything artistic. Art, in America, seems to give way to self-promotion, and self-promotion itself becomes *the* art form. One need no longer create any specific type of content; simply to be a 'content creator' ticks the box, marks one as a creative, perhaps even an artist, at the expense of any actual art *form*. Of course, some art forms blur the line: dance, for instance, can mean many things. On the internet, however, addiction impulse reigns supreme, and one's artistic or creative reach can be directly correlated to their sex appeal.

The third method of coping with the metacuration platforms of the internet is less an interaction, by degrees, with those platforms, as a reaction to them. Those platforms constitute a menace, an existential threat to the entire idea of creating anything at all. Many creatives, I believe, respond reflexively to this menace by hypercreating—by compulsively creating in bewildering volume, in a conscious or semiconscious attempt to counteract their own perceived artistic insignificance. It's a Sisyphean reaction, but also an honest, downright American one.[3] David versus Goliath, in a sense—if Goliath were the size of a galaxy, rather than a slightly larger man.

To provide an extreme example, Viper the Rapper, an outsider-artist-rapper, released 345 albums in 2014, and another 262 in 2015. To date of this writing (in 2020), Viper has released over a thousand albums. Without dissecting these statistics for quality, industry standards (e.g., number of songs per album), or other specifics, we can still look at these numbers and sense the profound, ominous presence of the internet. Perhaps it has more to do with a lifetime of creation funneled through a few years; perhaps the prodigious output will taper off, will reveal itself as a flash flood rather than a Biblical one. There are compulsive producers from other times, too—Marcel Proust, Harry Darger— but Viper's output is of a higher order, truly *internetian*; it is a scale of individual creation wholly of the internet era, and none other.

---

[3]Which is to say, a *productivity-oriented* reaction.

Enter Slikk: another rapper of prodigious output. He is so prolific he does not even know how many albums or mixtapes he has released.[4] Although on an understandably smaller scale, and at half Viper's age—and with a much keener eye to quality on a song-by-song basis—Slikk's twenty-odd solo albums, twenty-odd collaborative albums, and his hundreds upon hundreds of collaborations and singles boggle the mind. Slikk is relentlessly consistent and manages, for the most part, to be relentlessly transgressive. Of course, as soon as I assert this, exceptions come to mind. Qualified exceptions—such as those tracks that have persisted through an evolution to Slikk's mature phase of musical production, tracks which feel developmental, immature. I would lump a great deal of his work with Metro Zu in this category, as many of those tracks have a sophomoric feel to them. Not that there aren't gems—and not that all of Metro Zu's albums should be included as part of a category of juvenilia—but I sense collabora-

---

[4]As he admits in the interview with The Mars Files (21:10-21:15).

tion, the work of Metro Zu done largely with Slikk's brother (the rapper Lofty305) laying the groundwork for what will become a distinct style and method in later solo work.

But let's get back to the consequences of relentless output. The internet creates in some artists a compulsive need to create a body of work quickly—to have a volume of music to offset the immensity of the volume of existing music. There is also, with social media, a proliferation of supposedly DIY celebrity—those 'celebrities' who have, by the curation of their own or others' content, risen to a level of reknown. This can, I think, add to an artist's anxiety about creation. Maybe they see it like this: in their idols who came of age and built their celebrity before the advent of the internet age, there is already a volume of work—a life's work—presented on a personal webpage, or a fanpage, or somewhere online that constitutes a sizable presence for such an artist. They may appear, by a lifetime's artistic labors, to have made respectable room for themselves within a few genres they inhabit. This may all be illusory, of course, insofar as our means of perception hail from a pre-internet world, for the understanding *of* a pre-internet world. So we may see one of our idols—Tom Petty, let's say, or Method Man—as a titan within a genre, one who comes up with some healthy frequency on a playlist, and the perception of this level of success might translate in the mind of a young artist as a respectable level of success among internet-based artistic platforms. Not true. For those who've made their careers pre-internet, or despite the internet, an online presence is incidental and likely produces only a negligible return to the artist. They make their money elsewhere by more traditional means: touring, record sales. Only at the highest levels, and then, still, mostly among superstars or the younger anointed (and industry manufactured) pop icons is real money made primarily online, and only when one has millions upon millions of plays.

Celebrity, Pornography, and Transgression

There is always that nagging promise of internet celebrity, which can tug at a young artist; the idea, the *possibility* of becoming self-made through one's own clever content on Instagram or TikTok or Youtube. Much of this is, of course, illusory. The problem begins with the disintegrated notion of celebrity. What once was a product of advertising, acceptable-to-remarkable performance of talent within mainstream projects, and the requisite minimums of beauty in an average or standard sense, has become something that possessors of one or two of these qualities can seize for themselves through supposedly-democratizing social media. An artist, say, who possesses a better-than-average, standardly beautiful body can deploy it cleverly on Instagram to farm clicks and views, and build for themselves a private army of admirers. Translating that kind of attention to the selling of art, however, can prove tricky. To some degree, this kind of digital self-selling—a form of sex work, really—has become its own creative pursuit within the social media genres of "modeling," or "fitness," or, more nebulously, "content creation."

Of course, some of these practitioners are artistic in their creations. Some merely practice a form of packaging—a kind of self-curation for others' easy consumption. It's another platform where genre is crucial. Just as there is an incredibly broad spectrum of artistic quality within the genre of "dance," there are broad ranges in all social media genres. "Fitness" can mean anything from a world-class fit marathon runner, shotputter, or triathlete—truly a full-time athlete, a professionally fit person—to a gym rat who has muscle but loses his breath after the slightest jog; a model, essentially, whose content consists of the public advertising of sponsored clothing. The range also includes, of course,

professionalism—from those lives of professional ath-
letes made available for the passive consumption of the
interested public (and potential sponsors), to the ama-
teur who merely craves the attention of strangers. The
common denominator for popularity—for the existence, or nonexistence of 'celebrity'—may be the personal beauty, or sympathetic appeal of the individual in
question.

The pursuit of nebulous celebrity can lead an artist
to branch into social media content creation, over and
above the pursuit of art-making. A painter might start
out logically, by posting digital photographs of their
paintings to an Instagram account: the visual appeal of
a painting finds a place in a visual medium. But to find
an audience, this is never enough. From pictures of
paintings, she might graduate to short videos of herself
painting pictures—or time-lapse footage of the painting
of a picture. Art, like music, must become entertainment for it to stand out; as music is heard everywhere

and almost never listened to, thus is art frequently seen and rarely observed.

An artist might try and curate a digital walkthrough of a personal exhibit of their work—a story, both pictures and video—but all of this becomes something more than or apart from the original art, to which the artist has, we hope, still devoted their most precious hours. Suddenly, the artist's content inevitably eats into their time making art; very likely, this aspect of their public persona building has become more important than their actual art-making. Is this really a problem? Only for people practicing pre-internet forms of artistry. For those whose canvas *is* the cell phone screen, and whose payment is, or derives from, clicks and swipe-throughs, the activity of self-promotion is the art form. Not yet, but someday, perhaps, all art will begin and end with various forms of self-marketing.

Until then, the pull of achieving some modicum of digital celebrity, however small, will take time away from an artist's necessary, concrete, and seemingly old-fashioned pursuit of art-making. How to balance the two? If one has *only* to make art and manage one's own digital presence, perhaps there is plenty of time. If one has to do both of these things as well as sell one's labor for money—in order to live—it could be too much. There is something to be said of those who ignore social media altogether and simply make art, and pursue non-digital channels for the promoting, sharing, and showing of their art. If one can succeed this way, social media attention might follow; it might even be inevitable. If everyone around you has a cell phone and is constantly curating their own social media, why must the artist be required to do the exact same?

And another question: what constitutes celebrity, if the term has become so democratized and degraded? Is it 100,000 followers on Instagram? Is that a possible minimum definition of celebrity? Is it a certain quantity of likes, a certain minimum level of subscribers—that is, professed *devoted* fans, who may be counted on to consume every and all content which is uploaded? Is the promise of an audience the marker, or the result of celebrity? Is celebrity notoriety, infamy, of fame? Are these still different, or are they all the same? In the era of the leaked nude, sextape, 'broken' scandal, and so on, perhaps there really is no difference: fame is fame, celebrity is celebrity. Attention is both bad and good, all at the same time. Fame means both a target on one's back as well as a ring to kiss. If, at one point in our history, we might have pitied a famous person for having a dangerous stalker or an aggressive paparazzo, now fame seems only to elicit simply different shades of envy, from admiration-envy to resentment-envy. It's all bad, and all good, and it all seems to come from the same place of calculated exposure, whether it's painstakingly negotiated, compensated, and presented on a film screen, or it's leaked, intended or not, and shared: a new form of knowledge, perhaps even of negotiable tender; a public secret.

I see in Ruben Slikk's career trajectory not only compulsive artistic creation, and the anxiety implicit in such frenetic activity, but another kind of anxiety—the anxiety about successfully building, achieving, and exploiting celebrity. *How*, for instance, is Slikk famous? *Where* is Slikk famous? Is he famous from his shocking lyrics or from his Walgreens burglary? Does he draw fame from his incarceration—and attendant mugshot, much shared online—or from his brushes with those further along than he in their own pursuits of fame: Denzel Curry, Lil Peep (RIP), Riley Reid, and the like? He has few songs with *many* views, or "listens." He has many dozens more songs with a respectable thousand-or-so listens. He has a few Youtube videos with over 100,000 views. Did he think, upon seeing the very first of his videos miraculously falling upwards into the six figures, that his life would suddenly change? His newer singles, some of his very best, don't even have 1,000 views apiece. But that volume—the fact that he has *hundreds* of videos on Youtube in addition to hundreds of songs—does *that* matter? Does it matter that he has many millions of views, scattered across many hundreds of different videos, hundreds of different, individual creations? The fact that his music is on every known platform, to varying degrees of completeness, also is bewildering. How can an artist be in charge of their own work? How can a label, even? To keep track of it all may, in fact, be impossible, if we are truly to respect the true, *internetian* meaning of that tiny word: *all.*

So, then, what is fame? What is celebrity? A friend of mine, an artist whom I've known for a long time, once told me that he "doesn't believe in celebrity." That is maybe a good strategy. In the end, celebrities exist *as celebrities* because fans *believe* in them in the same way people believe in angels.[5] Without a belief in the possibility of fame, of the possibility of another human risen to a realm beyond the ordinary, that risen person becomes just another person whose feet touch the

---

[5]Or, for instance, the American dream, which continues to persist because people continue to believe that their own hard work and perseverance will eventually redeem them.

cold, filthy earth; who is saddled, day-by-day, with the same uninteresting inner monologue, the same aches and pains and doubts. Celebrities may run in circles of similarly revered, beautiful people, but they are all themselves believers; they believe they are special, and thus do they consort, and self-sort, exactly how we would expect celebrities to. It is a contract agreed to by all—celebrities, socialites, fans, paparazzi, promoters, agents, and so on, who are all part of the religion of celebrity, festooned in what we have been shown to be the life of the famous: camera flash, red carpets, velvet ropes, bouquets of microphones, and countless outlets hungry to record their follies and prosaic mumblings.

But this, too, is a bit old-fashioned. Celebrities aren't all movie stars, and certainly social media has created a kind of celebrity, that, if anything, requires even more strained belief, since we often cannot, or do not, see social media celebrities outside of their chosen media, as their celebrity comes simply from their talent for flawless navigation and exploitation of the online persona within the parameters of one or two social media platforms. A better question might be: is someone who masters Instagram really famous? Possibly not. Are they 'a' celebrity? Perhaps they are more like cult leaders, whom you or I may never have heard of, but for the hundred thousand "fans" they "have," they most certainly belong shoulder-to-shoulder with, say, Brad Pitt or Lady Gaga (once again, I show my age!).

The relentless creativity, the relentless creation of accounts on various social media and music sites—the anxiety, the heart-wrenching thirst for attention, for fame, for *celebrity*—may push Slikk, like many other young artists, to extremes. It must exact a cost—but it must feel, for many, like the only possible route to fame, or remuneration—or both.

Recently, in what I would characterize as a bid to propagate his public persona—and perhaps out of a drying up of other sources of remuneration—Slikk has made the jump to mainstream pornography. While he has produced gonzoish, murkily pornographic music videos, sporting nudity, sex acts, showing genitalia but not lingering on it, this move to mainstream pornography is telling, and actually makes plenty of sense for the public persona Slikk has cultivated over the years. How is it different? First, they aren't music videos, and while the visuals in his earlier forays into the pornographic might have outdone or overwhelmed the music to which they were attached, the music was still the point—it was the song that was being adorned, rather than the luminous and pulsating figures on screen being adorned by the music. This is crucial. The other thing this jump-to-porn signals is a level of assertion; that the persona Slikk has worked to create is deserving of a certain kind of worship. The production ticks a box under a category of narcissism that points to a robust self-belief in his own celebrity. In a way it is proof of a kind of tithing, of belonging to the religion of celebrity. What awaits is the realization of the fanbase, perhaps by industry professionals, that they have a true believer on their hands, someone who will do what is necessary to continually affirm their beliefs. This can mean big bucks—not necessarily that it *will* mean big bucks, but it that *can, might, could.* It is my prediction that Slikk's jump to mainstream pornography presages jumps across to other mainstream genres. This would, of course, dilute the transgressiveness of his music; a jump to mainstream pop music might in fact complete-ly *negate* or *refute* the transgressive in his work altogeth-er—for it would mean that rather than his work exist-ing as a transgression of norms, it becomes those norms—or, at the very least, becomes an accepted stop along the path towards what is normal, acceptable, sta-tus quo, even quotidian. The vulgar, the excessive, the viscerally abrasive—these aspects of Slikk's music, in the wake of wholesale mainstreaming, would be written off as juvenilia: the rantings and ravings of a resentful failure before, without, or envious of success as those in the mainstream understand it. Capitalism, if it can figure out a way, will eat even its own discontents and dissenters—those who have made a concerted effort to operate outside of its dictates—if it can reach them.

Pornography is, of course, a real darling of capitalism, one of a few essential, and marvelously successful legal yokings of addiction to the ruthless pursuit of profit. Like the market-flooding of Purdue Pharma, or the pumping of pop music into commercial spaces, pornography has risen above its associated stigmas by dint of its sheer capitalistic promise. It's among the greatest of industries, on par with the NFL or VIACOM, depending on how one defines its parameters. Perhaps it is a stretch to say that Ruben Slikk has made a jump to *mainstream* pornography, but indeed, overall, in the past decade, porn has made massive strides into the mainstream, full-stop. While there will always be fringes and subcultures of it, pornography is a big part of pop culture. Porn may never overcome all of its stigma (which would require, in effect, a complete repudiation of religious prudishness, perhaps of organized religion itself), but most people are aware, by now, just what an eminence grise porn is.

Another interesting thing about Slikk's move is that, despite the heteromaximal nature of his persona, his early forays into porn were in the male-focused genre. Not homosexual, exactly—his costar is a woman—but male-focused, as in, the camera most definitively lingers on Slikk and not the woman. This fits the narcissistic construct of Ruben Slikk–as-persona, as a fictionalized version of the self, a liberated *id*, but, indeed, at this point borders begin to be crossed: the heteromaximal, bent to the extreme, bends back around, begins to shade homoerotic again. It makes sense, when we realize who it is, throughout the oeuvre; and what the sex means: who is being supplicated to, who's being edified, where the confirmation of power lies. Who it is, in effect, we are being asked to worship.

Slikk addresses cult leadership often in his music. He draws a clear link between cult leadership and pimping—and, by extension, the Jesus-Christ-assuperpimp trope of much of his work. He identifies and celebrates the fact that idolization is inherently sexual, and, by extension, that sexuality is inherently worshipful. To the extent that sexuality can tend towards fixation—either on an individual or, more generally, on particular body parts of the attractant sex—it does begin to appear very fetishistic, in the original meaning of that word, especially in an age of visual addiction, an age where what we wish to gaze upon *can* be gazed upon, usually within a matter of seconds. Thus do we create altars of such fetishes, or generalized notions of the parts of a whole concept of sex which stand out as the primary erotic accelerant.

In literature we get the word 'sex' itself used as a euphemism for the vagina—e.g. "He cupped her sex with his hand"—the word *sex* becoming a synechdoche for the entire *sex organ*. Further, vagina—rather its vulgar colloquial form, 'pussy'—has become a synechdoche for the entirety of sexual interaction, for all of *sex*. In Slikk's oeuvre, the focus is on Slikk's penis—

once again, another way in which homoeroticism inevitably creeps into the heteromaximal. Sex cannot exist in such a narrow focus, of course; but sex organs, *parts* of a person, can be sexually fetishized, and worshipped. It could be fair to ask, then, whether sex is the right word to use. Many of Slikk's lyrics deal in body parts, and seem to be in an erotic, fetishistic, worshipful mode— the obsession over female body parts—rather than dealing in sexuality itself, which requires human beings, interaction, the co-conspiring of erotically charged minds.

But maybe such a linguistic dissection misses the point; maybe it's too sober an inquiry. Something Slikk—and, to some degree, perhaps, contemporary gangsta rap culture—has in common with pornography is the presentation of unfettered hyperbole. Of *outlandishness*. The presentation of maximal fantasies, or maximal distortions of reality, really contortions to oxymoronic extremes, which can end up being quite nearly a critique of those very same fantasies.

To portray a contortion of desire—with all the trappings of desire—pushed to extremes is to accelerate a utopian vision well past its prime, well past its moment of utopia to the point that it's gone decadent and become a burden and a degeneration of its own inhabitants, its own purveyors. That such a thing can yet be presented as an idea of utopia and consumed as a discreet unit simply highlights its own transience—that such suggestions of utopia cannot so much be lived as expended, used up. True utopia, of course, is unattainable.

As a form of staged utopia, pornography is not innocent by any means, but neither are any utopias. All require, for their achievement, the debasing, dehumanizing, or at the very least the deferral of others' preferred harmonies, in order to exist. Utopias are always ideas, therefore they come from individuals, or, at best, small groups of people. There has never been a utopian vision which fits *all* people, though many utopias purport to be, or *to have been*, universal. It is simply an impossible ask: a utopia that satisfies everybody's needs. Maybe it is not possible. Certainly for extreme utopian constructions, there are no suggestions that such situations are a satisfaction to all. At best, a few are satisfied and the many are left alone; at worst, the satisfaction of the few necessarily *requires* the debasing of the many. Capitalism is one version of this latter kind of (supposed) utopia, and it's experiencing a long overdue period of disaffection. Most people don't want their own harmony to have to come at the expense of others', as a sense of guilt taints one's sense of harmony. The striving for societal utopia has in the past been preceded, and succeeded, by inhuman terrors, mass murder, and the like. So to carefully delineate it, and describe a singular unit of utopia—just one purveyor's absurd notion of it—is to acknowledge the destructiveness and the danger of utopia, while also celebrating it as sheer fantasy.

Art, Entertainment, and Laziness

Transgressive art cannot exist in a vacuum; cannot indeed exist without its detractors present to make clear, to everyone, how exactly it is transgressive and where, and when, the artist happened to have crossed a line. Utopia works in the same way. Without someone there to sound the alarm, without the reflexive shock of realizing that someone, or some system, has flown too close to the sun, a utopia cannot be said to have been striven for, let alone achieved.

In the past, utopias could only be conveyed through writing, speech, or paintings. To be able to visually represent utopia with film had an immediate effect: the invention of film and the debut of motion-picture pornography are near simultaneous. What comes after, what *came* after, is a negotiation, a reaction:

censors for the medium of film materialized to address this new problem: to identify obscenity and to proscribe it. They did not succeed in defining it; to define pornography has remained, to this day, a near-impossible task. I, of course, am doing so; defining pornography as a presentation of individual, subjective utopia. It remains to be seen if utopia, in the conventional sociopolitical sense, will ever so much as *seem* attainable. There have only ever been individual or small-group schematics of utopia which are then imposed forcibly upon societies. Societies thus imposed upon can achieve only approximations of functionality—something, anything *but* utopia: sheer disaster, chaos. A 'functioning utopia,' then, is an oxymoron. A working society might be, in its most mature iteration, an antithesis to utopia.

So, then, when it comes to transgressive creations, transgressive cultural artifacts which articulate only one individual's notion of utopia, the issue might be whether or not such a creation should be considered art.

Someone who consumes enough music by Ruben Slikk eventually cannot but see a level of preposterousness to it, in the relentlessness of the absurd gesture, in the world building around the persona that is Ruben Slikk. It's not altogether ridiculous, of course; there are moments of mildness, if one looks closely enough; periods of meditation separate manic periods of cannibalistic sexual excess—musical refractory periods, in a sense. It's not unlike many other kinds of commercially viable—meaning, ultimately, capitalist—rap, but the intensity of the manic periods rise to such a height that, in Slikk's case, the music ceases to be commercial, or simply cannot be.

Slikk's uncommercializability is an admirable quality, as commercialization rarely uplifts an art object any further than it has reached on its own merit. Often enough, even the entry of an art object into a commercial realm comes with—can *only* come with—a degradation of some kind, a reduction of some quality of it, or of the object as a whole.[6] The artist *sells out*, has become a *sellout*. They might lose critical credibility, or credibility among their peers, especially if those peers come from an as-yet "unsuccessful" milieu. This is a stigma primarily in artistic subcultures, which hold a higher standard of artistic integrity than that of the mainstream. Once again, the subculture that comes to mind is punk rock.

But I think a sensitivity to the degrading power of commercialization should apply across the board, if we want to continue to believe that there is indeed such a thing as authentic art. We absolutely must put to rest the old, self-affirming notion that, for lack of a better set of criteria, commercial viability—the "objectivity" of the free market—is the best measure of artistic quality. I don't think I have to get into this too much; as the

---

[6]This then, is another tenet of cultural anarchism: that capitalist systems and institutions are anathema to art. Art, in order to remain artistic, must avoid qualities that appeal to those systems. Slikk's uncommercializability is a virtue, as part of what he is doing in his art repulses those systems.

internet ages and putrefies, I think it has become all too clear that the greatest popularity comes from the greatest financial input, or a calculated deployment of least common denominators, or, most successfully, a mix of both. If we don't want our culture reduced to such basics—and I do mean *basics*, the basest of the basic—we must take it for granted that *not only* must art be completely unbeholden to commerce, it must be understood that art is categorically *denatured, reduced, damaged* by too much association with commerce. Money taints all things, yes—*mo' money, mo' problems*—but art suffers especially in its company.

The only forms of art which seem immune to the negative effects of commerce are those which are so old that they have survived many generations' worth of critical appraisal. Of course, this makes such classics of the canon—Picasso's works; but also those of Rembrandt and his ilk, and Beethoven, Mahler, Hildegaard von Bingen: *old art indeed*—less interesting, and utterly 'safe': the fate of anything which becomes a standard, an exemplar, and is hung in a museum. Those aspects of the classics which once may have been transgressive—the way Stravinsky's music used to send people into a riot—are exceedingly difficult to perceive, to reclaim, to explain, and to convey, and the burden of explanation of those merits falls witheringly to specialists. Contemporary art has context by which it can be measured. Anything unusual, or unique, or ingenious will always suffer in a commercial meritocratic environment, which sees profit (thus, quality) in the averaging mechanisms which favor the basest basic—the addiction-impulse consumption of the internet and social media—and so prizes addictiveness over any other measure. For this reason, all the beautiful and strange outliers who do not comfortably fit preset categories described by metacuration engines such as Spotify need to be championed by critics, ideally critics who are not associated with sales—who are not advertorial mercenaries, but are in some way voluntarily detached. Academics can suffice, insofar as the stigma of academic critique does not harm the process, but independent peer-artists would be better. DIY zine culture—and by degrees the mostly online written culture that has sprung up around soundcloud rap, to attempt to describe and understand it—is moving closer to an ideal, as it comes to the game professedly anti-establishment, and anti-commercial. The point of such peer-to-peer critical interpretation is to spread the word about those works and their creators who have not benefitted or cannot benefit from the commercial meritocracy. Further, the point of peer-to-peer DIY critical culture is to determine what's actually worthwhile and what's not—what's art and what's dreck—to have, in short, a naturally-occurring, built in bullshit-detector. The punk rock aversion to selling out ought to translate to soundcloud rap. This is not the case with most rap, of course, just as it isn't the case with most music, which by and large *seeks* commercialization, seeks to turn a profit and become attractive as a means by which many different parties—not just the so-called 'artist,' and his label, but also intermediaries and sponsors—can earn money.

Now, it might very well be the case that Ruben Slikk seeks mainstream remuneration for his artistic output. It's not out of the question, of course. While this desire might run counter to the punk rock ethos I'm arguing for—that he would rather make fat stacks rather that have some nebulous artistic 'cred'—it matters less, I think, to a critical understanding of the artist and his intentions with the building of an oeuvre. Working artists—as opposed to those who are merely attempting to satisfy a commercial demand—ought to be building a master narrative with their oeuvre. Frank Zappa—another musician/artist who trod the line between the popular and the transgressive—called this 'conceptual continuity,' and argued that he considered all his work, every album and song, every piece of music he ever made to be part of a singular whole. If commercial demands and pure remuneration had been the first priority, then I think at some point, perhaps between albums twelve and twenty-two, Slikk might have decided to water things down in the hopes of attracting the interest of a label or some kind of intermediary salesperson. But, by and large, there is no such swerve. Here and there I think one can detect a deviation towards the commercial, towards the mainstream. "These Streets" seems to be one—a one-off single which has only the barest connection to Slikk's larger body of work. It feels like an attempt by the artist, with or without outside influence, to appeal to commercial entities. Especially coming out between, indeed *among* a whole string of singles released on YouTube and elsewhere which are wholly within Slikk's own built context—his own set of criteria of relentless assault on the mores of pop music, its clichés and idioms, gratuities, boredoms, banalities—all those pathetic bits and pieces which he spears through track by track, using his own tweaks to a formula to pump the grit back into popular music. It is not, of course, 'popular,' but it comes in that mode, with a lot of the familiar sounds and tricks and noises of contemporary pop. Lyrically, there is great violence—great rage towards the wasted decibels of radio pop—but I'm getting ahead of myself. The point is that "These Streets" feels like an exception, a renunciation of Slikk's conceptual continuity.

It does not mean that remuneration is not deserved, or has not, through years and years of work, been *earned*. As with many artists and academics, the hours are long indeed, and the rewards few. Slikk has produced work an order of magnitude greater than most of the best rappers—indeed most of the best musicians, generally speaking, worldwide. While time spent or volume of output can inevitably become, in the estimations of many, corollaries to a capitalistic measure of 'productivity,' there can be artists who nonetheless achieve remuneration outside of the artistically destructive system of commercial meritocracy. Many achieve this through difficult, time-consuming person-to-person work: traveling and touring, suffering privations and foregoing the comforts of an ordinary life. Deep into the age of the internet, some regard for this approach has been lost, as the numerical outliers of internet-to-stage pop stardom have been presented to us as the most efficient, economical, or sometimes *only* way to achieve acclaim and some degree of remuneration as a musician. Those who earn money as part of the music industry would like us to think these ordinary, long-shot methods are the best methods. They want us to put our heads down and play the awful game. They are wrong: DIY touring and arduous person-to-person 'networking'—i.e. being human, being friendly, sharing one's passion—might still be the best, most direct pathway to remuneration through one's music. It might take some time for this to reveal itself again, especially with the industry so totally invested in its own persistence.

Most people know that music made with a few cheap microphones and a couple of decent software programs can come within a hair's width of radio quality—the biggest factor being the vision and the talent of the artist herself. Has this democratization of the means to produce also become a nail in the coffin of remuneration? If everyone can make something *basically* as good as what's on the radio, what has prevented artists and peers, by and large, from renouncing commercial pop music? Laziness, I would say; people hear what's on the radio, because it's pumped at them in commercial settings—the grocery store, waiting rooms, hold lines, elevators—and, most insidiously, combined with alcohol and the potential for self-edification and possible sex, it is blasted into peoples' eardrums in clubs and bars. Popular music is made to sell things, so when someone makes it on a laptop and asks someone else to consume it, outside of these passive contexts, walls tend to come up. Not always, of course, but often, because of the entwined nature of pop music and commerce, and how it must feel like doing something for nothing (a capitalism no-no), for a potential listener to *consider* music outside of these commercial contexts, to *listen* to it rather than to hear it, to feel it—ultimately, to actively *not* listen to it—while more important activities—spending money, self-inebriating, seeking sex—are carried out. Slikk's oversexualized, descriptive, sometimes disgusting lyrics pull the veil from the subject of sex in carefully dressed-up club music, from pop music in general. It's all about sex, it's all about *fucking*, but to reduce it to a ruggedly anatomical level is to bring to the fore a near-atavistic sexuality, stripped of theoretical love—as in pop music, as in club music—stripped of the ultimately conservative push-and-pull of love games, of downright prudish negotiations of relationship and sexual politics. No—it's all beside the point, and just reinforces societal conservatism around the ideas of sex, about its titillating, thus naughty, thus *taboo*, thus *sinful* nature: sexuality in a Slikk tune is strictly the conjuring of pleasure, the usage of flesh to an almost mediocre, petty end. But that is what most pop music is about, it is just that pop music, by and large, is too beholden to commercial standards, to the achieving of remuneration—and then the continuous maintenance of it—to be truly blunt, truly fresh, truly revolutionarily open about sexuality.

In the suppression of desire, money can be continuously made. The suggestion of sex, of the execution of the sex act as a transgression—sex as sin—is a conservative notion, through and through, but within the simple idea of sin there is an endless river of money to tap into. The recipe is always the same: endless permutations of suggestive lyrics; swooping melodies; voices cracking into falsetto to suggest or evince orgasm—an attainment of heaven, of one's fantasy, one's utopia— all undergirded by a very strict tempo; a narrow range of beats-per-minute; and a bare handful of synthesized sounds. Near-interchangeably these ingredients are collected to reproduce an aversion to sex, an idea of a need for a certain kind of sex, a revulsion of one's own desire (because it's naughty, therefore filthy, therefore sinful), and, ultimately, a diminishment of self-worth. When we feel this way—less than whole—capitalism can swoop in and sell us just the thing to make us feel

whole again, at least temporarily, and the cycle

continues…

The Humorlessness of Pop Music

It's a serious business, the manipulation of people in order to soften them, to make them receptive to and ready to consume. So serious is this venture, in fact, that popular music rarely ever contains humor or levity.[7] The attitude of popular music can sometimes be less than serious—it can sometimes be lax, or easy-going—but it is almost never *funny*. It's difficult to be funny in music, for one thing; more importantly, however, laughter is antithetical—or at least irrelevant—to consumption. *Coolness*,[8] not humor, is a much more efficient tool for selling. To convey *cool*, which is to say, to convey *enviability*, is the primary purpose of popular

---

[7]The same can be said about popular literature and literary fiction in the United States, but for very different reasons.

[8]And I would define "cool" as the portrayal, or condition, of eliciting envy or desire in the observer.

music and all promotional auxiliaries that accompany it. Music videos produced for popular songs only ever employ humor as a secondary, recapitulatory means of emphasizing their own enviability, their own cool. Mostly, straight *cool* is enough: relaxed attitudes; unsmiling, self-assured natures—often of aroused women and indifferent men, or the opposite, if the popstar is a woman—and always surrounded by enough comfort and luxury to relax and imbue confidence in even the most insecure celebrity.

Laughter, however, cures too many of these ills of addiction and excess; it cuts right through the anxious and insecure feelings that cause one to be envious, and to consume in order to remedy those feelings.

And so, another question: can popular music, if it is beholden to commerce, ever be anything short of self-serious? Can it ever be actually *funny*? If music can be comic, *where* can it be comic? *When*, in a piece of music, can comedy *occur*? The most obvious answer might be in the lyrics, meaning that in order to engage with the humor one has to get past the façade, to be won over to bother to listen, long before any humor can be gleaned from the piece of music itself. For, if the humor is in the lyrics, the humor lies *inside* the song. Sometimes humor, or comedy, or the levity in a piece of music exists outside the song—in its titling or artwork—or in the cultivated persona of the artist herself. Sometimes there lies humor, or jokes, of a kind, in the very notes of the music, but for many this can be especially hard to realize, as people have a broad and varied relationship to sound[9]: what 'sounds' funny to one person might not to another. Songs, poems, rhymes with dirty—thus, comedic, or light—lyrics are as old as time. Traditional dirty limericks, the poems of Ovid and Catullus, and Goethe's *Venetian Epigrams*—these are all famous examples of what had to be an omnipresent form: bawdy, funny, short rhymes common folk would

---

[9]As well as to compositional norms, where subversion of one or a few of those norms might constitute a kind of humor or joke on the form itself.

memorize to make their tavern fellows laugh—all forms of popular entertainment which may or may not require musical accompaniment. To make a point, *opera buffa* and *operetta* came about as lighter alternatives to opera, which was understood to be high art. Shakespearan Comedy, not to mention the works written by a thousand popular and competent others, also used the same methods to achieve humor—double entendre, innuendo, implication, slapstick and so on—to entertain and to remain popular for centuries after their composition.

But in contemporary music, there seem to be three areas where humor can have an affect—indeed, where any message can land home, if there is a message to deliver. The first is in the title of a piece of music. Frank Zappa's "I Promise Not to Come in Your Mouth," is an instance where a humorous or provocative title is applied to an instrumental jazz-fusion piece which otherwise might not be particularly notable or meaningfully differentiated from other pieces like it.

Among Frank Zappa's work, there are many examples of the funny title for an otherwise not-all-that-funny piece of music, but there is no doubt that the title, as it is typically encountered before the music, works to affect the music itself. Aware of the title, one searches the music, as it comes, for some confirmation of what the title promises. As in music, as in literature. In popular music, the title is often too obvious, and there is no searching necessary. Sometimes it's like the title is there exclusively for filing purposes and quick reference rather than an opportunity to finalize, round-off, aggrandize or otherwise enhance the work.

The second place humor can exist is in the artwork. Frank Zappa squeezes as much as he can from his album art. Ruben Slikk, as an ideological descendant of the great satirizer Zappa, does the same. Perhaps Slikk's albums are less a satirization of society than of the persona-self, but maybe not. The self is never really isolated from society, and if Slikk's main purpose is to exist within a larger context of hip-hop/rap—or, simply, pop music—then there are most certainly elements of society recapitulated, commented upon, skewered, in the art itself. There is a lot at play; elements of internet culture, emojis, gonzo pornography, *de rigeur* rap culture (e.g. pistols, fat stacks of cash, jewelry, drugs), folk or outsider or "primitivist" art elements—e.g. Microsoft Paint or graffiti strokes—and so on. The overall effect could be said to be Afrofuturist, and Slikk's presentation of his persona-self is similarly so—psychedelic, colorful, outrageous in a way similar to many current underground rappers—more playful, funnier, less serious than many successful rappers of the previous generation, where a relentless presentation of *cool*, sometimes in the form of brand representation (sought or actual sponsorship) and conspicuous wealth were dominant operative modes, with only a little wiggle room otherwise for personal differentiation, humor, or notable individuation.[10] So, in addition to many of Slikk's

---

[10]I wonder if this has to do with when different generations came of age. The 90s rap scene came of age during Reagan-Bush, which

titles being a continuation of his overall conceptual world-building—and, indeed, language building, for he has created his own unique vocabulary and language in and through his rapping[11]—and a source of humor, his album and single covers are a collage of references, satirical one-offs, suggestive gifs and memes, and shock tableaux. Beyond that, his titling has, over the years,

---

could have really blunted any levity in their artmaking process. Compare that to Slikk, who came of age during the Obama administration, and may have felt freer to be goofy, playful, and perhaps more in opposition to the music industry than to political elites, systemic economic injustice and the like.

[11]To illustrate this with but a scant two neologisms which Slikk has himself explicitly defined, in his own words:

Fishmixxx—"Fishmixxx can be really anything; a mixture of different drugs that you take at the same time, or the estrogen that you extract from the female during intercourse, and, you know, it could be two different…varieties of estrogen…or several different varieties of estrogen, depending on how much vagina you penetrate at that point in time" (The Mars Files interview, 18:02-18:30).

Bisquikk [beesqueeck?]—"Bisquikk is basically being addicted to codeine cough syrup, and um, it's basically like um, being absorbed into the codeine, you know? And also, you know, when you mix the bisquick, and the little, and the thang-thang, and then you pour it on the pan, and its just like—the wrist motion is skrr skrr ['skeet skeet']" (The Mars Files interview, 18:31-18:57). There are many others, but those two are possibly the most famous.

developed its own system of spelling, such that "ass," to take one example, has become "auhzz."[12] It's a phonetic kind of spelling which may have originated in slang—or, dare I use the paleologism *Ebonics*[13]—but has, over the years and albums, come to be more directly related to Slikk's own conceptual linguistics, perhaps in part an outgrowth of spelling idiosyncrasies in larger soundcloud-, weirdo-rap, and other *sub-rosa* internet communities. In an extreme era, the totality of Slikk's *oeuvre* stands up to meet those extremes. One cannot limit their intensity to the music itself, or the art itself, or the persona behind the art: it must show through everywhere, all the time, or people will fail to notice.

Another extreme of careful linguistic attention paid is Slikk's use of the *er*-suffixed N-word. It could be a shock value byproduct, of course; Slikk wants to shock

---

[12]As in the music video "Nicolette's Auhzzz" or the single, "Fohkenerauhzzzzz" available on YouTube.

[13]And, as Slikk has said himself: "I'm far too proper/to adhere to Ebonics" (1:51-1:54 in [*sic*] "N— of the Year").

as much as possible, and rap's near-universal deployment of the lighter *n—a* perhaps no longer is shocking. But a lot changes when one replaces *a* with *er*. Already, *n—* might possibly be the most powerful word in the English language, at least in American English, bringing to bear in six little letters the full force of four hundred years of brutality perpetrated on black people by whites, a violence which cannot be separated from its quintessentially capitalist impulse and the insane inhuman drive of that impulse to maximize profit at the expense of the lives of human beings. It might not be my place to delve into what that word can mean, but allow me to give it time of day, for just a moment, for the purposes of this essay.

A small part of this great violence is conveyed even in the softer *a*-suffixed version of the word. It cannot be avoided. In some way, I believe this little bit of invoked horror acts as a spice, adding a realistic tinge of luxury to the already decadent use of obscenity. I think that is its allure, for rap music, for black culture, perhaps, in a larger sense. I don't want to generalize where it's not my place, but it just seems like there is a lot of relish in the word's usage, as an indicator of camaraderie, a currency for shared experience or a kind of shared consciousness, be it race consciousness or class-consciousness, or some of both. Like all luxuries, which are in part luxurious because of the implicit component of exploitation contained in their production, to use the "n word"—something which, it is often said, must only be uttered by those within the community—is a kind of luxury, and without the horrific suffering of generations behind it, the word just wouldn't have the same power. To be a bit more grotesque, one might say that without all that suffering, the deployment of that word would lack its inborn taboo, and if the taboo is gone, so, too, is any act of transgression, or defiance, in the word's usage. Hard fought license indeed.

It is curious that a younger generation of underground rappers, many of whom are white, seem to use the *a*-suffixed version of the n-word with impunity. Is this simply a response to a general desensitization of our culture—that in order to appear *really badass*, they must cross a new line of transgression, one which previous generations might have seen as uncrossable? Could it also be a partial redirection of the word? To begin to use the word not when speaking derogatorily, or from within the community man-to-man, but when speaking of *anybody*? Would it not be a cultural game-changer to begin to call old white men *n*—*s*, whether in curse or jest? When young rappers of any color use the *a*-suffixed version among their own community—that is, the community of rappers, their friends, their peers—it might be part of a lengthy process of declawing the word, both the *a*- and *er*-suffixed versions.

Once upon a time, the white rapper was a novelty; nowadays, less so. Is this the mainstreaming of rap, or the whitening of it? Does the music-culture, as it has come down to us, supersede the black culture that gave it its form and scope in the first place? I would guess that no one asked permission; that some white rappers just started using the *a*-suffixed version of the word, and their black friends didn't say anything, or were genuinely okay with it.

I wonder.

To be rebellious, even against the inborn rebelliousness of rap music—to see oneself as a rebel against both mainstream culture *and* rap culture—might require this assumption of the form without permission, or, rather, this complete rewriting of the rules of the word's usage.

The same could be said about the R-word—*rape*—not really a swear word but a word which carries a similar unwieldy power. In an interview, when asked about the *RAPGAMERAPEMOBB* album, Ruben Slikk explained the "Rapemobb" "doesn't mean, like, sexually raping another human being, [but rather] it's like forcing your way into the rap game to make things work for you, in the best way possible"; that he and his will forthrightly impose their own will upon rap culture, that he will dominate and subordinate the 'rap game'—

he and his 'mobb,' his cohort of coconspirators.[14] I think it goes without saying that use of the word 'rape' is fairly contentious, and its usage in this instance is not without issue.

While so much music describes, celebrates, or otherwise *implies* rape, it is certainly a statement to blatantly use the r-word. Rape isn't even a profantity, but it does seem to have the same effect as some of the most intense four-letter words that can be thrown around. It might as well be, as it is among a very small group of words that, it seems, everyone in popular music, even in the semiautonomous subculture of rap music, has agreed not to use. The *-er* n-word, the r-word, and the c-word. Maybe the six-letter f-word as well.

The opening of this final box, the crossing of this final frontier by the most transgressive recording artists might signal a final twilight for obscenity as we understand it. Soon, if what they are making is ever to be

---

[14]From an interview with The Mars Files 13:50-14:09, available on YouTube (2016).

considered art, if it is ever to draw lasting cultural cachet from its shock value, it might very well *lose* that shock value over time, as all remaining avenues by which one might shock become closed. If using taboo words as one pleases is still shocking, it probably won't be for very much longer. If making explicitly pornographic music videos is shocking, that, too, will soon become commonplace. Ruben Slikk has a handful of songs whose titles (not to mention lyrics) deploy the *-er* suffixed n-word, and are intensified all the more by it. The shock value is keenly dialed in, dialed *up*. In the intro of "Sugar Cubes"—one of the best tracks on the *Jesus Boys* mixtape—there is a moment where he and Mike Dece are unisoning curse words in isolation—

Fucker...
N—...
Fucker...
N—...

—with Slikk whispering, in between, "Black man/I am a black man," and then "Swagger...!" before the chorus breaks in. What is the meaning of this? Slikk is clearly playing with sensitivities. *Where*, he might be asking, *does the obscenity lie?* Does it lie in the word itself, in isolation, or is it made offensive by its placement next to a seeming definition: "…I am a black man…," the words themselves lifted straight off a civil rights poster, a defiant declaring one's personhood, one's humanity. So, then as now—as ever, and always—the word is imbued with immeasurable power. It's very taboo that Slikk plays with it as much and as flagrantly as he does. And to whisper such tentatives, in between the words themselves: it's clear he's pranking, at least; that this particular cultural gibe is 100% intentional. Again, we must ask: is there value in such toying?

I would be remiss if I didn't at this point mention another shock-music group which, more than anything, relied on its titles—song and album—to cultivate a kind of humor in their work: Anal Cunt, a thrash-hardcore band from Allston, Massachusetts, which existed between approximately 1988 and 2010. Whether or not their overall concept was actually funny—rather than utterly insensate—depends on how generous, open-minded, or optimistic one wishes to be about them, about humanity in general. There is undoubtedly a self-conscious understanding of their own personae, of their own body of work as a kind of humorous or hyperbolic manifestation. With album titles such as *I Like it When You Die*, *40 More Reasons to Hate Us*, *Top Forty Hits*, and *It Just Gets Worse*, it is clear that the band—whose songs rarely top a minute, and whose albums, therefore, are typically 40-song eruptions of noise—understands what niche it has come to fill. On the level of the individual song, there is a keen sense of the punch line in titling. A whole series of titles in the second-person declarative mode are some of the funniest: "You Look Divorced," "You are an Interior Decorator," "You Have Goals," "You Look Adopted," "You Are a Food Critic," "You Live on a Houseboat," "You're Old (F*** You)," "You Own a Store," "You've Got No Friends," "Your Favorite Band Is Supertramp," "You _______ (Fill in the Blank)." These are charming, laddish, a bit insensitive but not all that bad. Here are a few more pretty funny titles that still seem to pass muster: "Valujet," "No, We Don't Want to Do a Split Seven Inch With Your Stupid Fucking Band," "Kyle From Incantation Has a Moustache," "Extreme Noise Terror Are Afraid of Us," "I Ate Your Horse," "Everyone in Allston Should be Killed," "I'm Really Excited About the Upcoming David Buskin Concert," "Being Ignorant is Awesome," "Don't Call Japanese Hardcore Japcore," "Morbid Dead Guy," "Hungry Hungry Hippos," "Breastfeeding Jim J. Bullock's Toenail Collection," "The South Won't Rise Again," "Jack Kevorkian is Cool," "Old Lady Across the Hall With No Life," "The Sultry Ways of Steve Berger," "Everyone in Anal Cunt is Dumb," "Everyone in the Underground Music Scene Is Stupid." If it ended there, it would be fairly funny—sophomoric, but relatively innocent. Unfortunately, they also evince the worst of their times. They are in fact bigoted; and their image has aged deservedly poorly. A sampling of the more cringeworthy: "Body by Auschwitz," "I'm Glad Jazz Faggots Don't Like Us Anymore," "You Went to See Dishwalla and Everclear (You're Gay)," "Laughing While Lennard Peltier Gets Raped in Prison," "I Pushed Your Wife In Front of the Subway," "Your Kid Committed Suicide Because You Suck," "I Sold Your Dog to a Chinese Restaurant," and so on. I have decided, if you can believe it, not to reproduce here the worst of their titles, but as bad as you can imagine, they have a song about it, probably five or ten. Anyway, the point is that one can cram some serious humor into a title, and rely on that, alone, to do a lot of work. While Anal Cunt reached for the heights of shock, and became over time fairly skilled at the art of the one-off punch line title, they ultimately were a pack of idiots who don't deserve much more than an eyebrow-raising passing mention. Their kind of outsider art is best left moldering in the slides bin, rather than put under the microscope.

Finally, the most standard means of injecting humor or satire into music: lyrics. With Slikk I get the sense that humor is the first intention—eliciting a laugh—and the secondary result, very possibly unintended, is the deep satirization of popular music and its nagging idioms. One example is the usage of 504 Boyz' track, featuring Mercedes, "I Can Tell," which in and of itself is fairly explicit. The refrain is:

> You ain't gotta say too much,
> From the look in your eyes I can tell you wanna
>   fuck.
> And you ain't gotta call me your boo,
> Just as bad as you wanna fuck I wanna fuck too.

Pretty great. Now, perhaps that song intrigued Slikk; perhaps he liked it a lot and drew inspiration from it. Needless to say, he had to make it his own, including the hiring of his own hook singer, his own Mercedes, to back his altered refrains:

> You ain't gotta say too much,
> Cause you know that Slikk's finna fuck you in the
>   butt.
> And you ain't even gotta use lube,
> Cos you know that Slikk's finna spit on his dick too.

Okay, so the original is hardly, in its own right, mainstream pop music. To be sure 504 Boyz and Mercedes might be only a hair's width closer to the mainstream than Ruben Slikk, but ultimately they are both a far cry from the Beyoncés, Adam Levines, and Taylor Swifts of the world. Still, the method of reproduction, with a twist, is the same. In many instances Ruben Slikk songs and singles are not particularly original. They sound a lot like pop songs and they have comparable bouncy, catchy beats and hooks. But, in this instance, where Slikk has literally taken all the component parts of another song, and simply amped up the lyrics, pushed them past the lustily sensual into the realm of the hilariously grotesque, the result is that the forms of the previous song are revealed in their simplicity, in their glibness, and—to the extent that they are self-serious (not so much with this particular song)—in their insincerity. In short, the original comes off as kind of commercial, even if it is edgily explicit. Honestly, I've nothing against 504 Boyz and Mercedes—this song is pretty great; a cult classic—but the point is that more popular, more commercial music deserves to be taken apart in this way, and revealed to be as vapid as it truly is.

Weird Al Yankovic gets away with this same satirical method. In fact, he could be said to be the most successful musical satirist of the last fifty years, in a class of his own. In part, his career has been helped by the fact that he has maintained a fairly good-natured, kid-friendly appeal. His satirizations of popular songs are always PG-13 at their raunchiest. ("Amish Paradise," for instance, is fairly sexual, but in that perfectly balanced way where a child might not catch it, but an adult can't possibly miss it.) Most of the time, Weird Al is straight-up G-rated. "Fat," as his remix of Michael Jackson's "Bad" is a good example. In a way, nearly all of the delight of the satire is drawn from the original— the music video directly copies the original, to say nothing of the song itself, which changes only the lyrical content. It's surprising that, with all the cultural capital Weird Al has, there has not been another musical satirist as successful. One-offs on Youtube are, of course, another story, as well as the autotune craze of the first decade of the millennium (also powered by Youtube), which saw a similar kind of satirical musicalization of nonmusical popular culture.

But it seems that few people have made the connection from Weird Al to the popular music he is making fun of. That those songs are simplistic and, at their best, manipulative. They tug at our heartstrings, *if* they tug at our heartstrings, by the employment of the most basic formulas of melody and content. You could say that they tug at our heartstrings by *literally tugging at our heartstrings*. They are churned out with the hopes that one or another will land home, will find a few sticking points amid the web of passive, latent culture, and someone will make some money.

The Gospel of Slikk and the Degradation of Art

And so we've come full-circle: the original sin of pop music is the recapitulation of the desires that drive capitalism. Often this recapitulation is unconscious, but it also seems hyperactivated in popular genres of music, where sponsorships beyond equipment related to the work of a musician or working artist are commonplace. The music, like television, is there to sell certain brands which reinforce a specifically curated lifestyle, that of the imagined rich and famous. For instance, it is possible that Megan Thee Stallion's message of empowerment might be undercut by the live presentation of her music, which emphasizes the objectification of the women performing, positing their bodies as *possibly* their greatest asset, but certainly their most emphasized one, at the exclusion of others. A supposedly liberated sexuality, so far as it is implied to be luxurious, inadvertently makes sexuality a commodity, and this makes the artist's message a fairly conservative one: the idea that sexuality, like a commodity, can be bought and sold, or traded, and might need to be regulated, too.

Along the same lines, if desire is somehow dangerous, as often it must be portrayed in order to sell something, desire itself becomes sinful—as sinful as conservative religious folk (for our purposes, Christians) have always maintained. And dangerous things—sinful things—must be controlled, *regulated*. That is, at least, the rationale for historical control of and restrictions put upon peoples' bodies. So, the message might appear liberating at first glance, but it is ultimately fraught, caught up in the demands of larger systems, of globalized western capitalism and conservative religious culture.

Slikk's antics are often gratuitous, but they are far too outrageous to be commodifiable in the same way, largely preventing commercialization of his message, as well as the interpretation of his focus as in any way conservative.[15] There is a certain amount of control retained in the apparent chaos.

Out of this one could lift, as a point of contention, the idea of Slikk's "message." What is his message? Does he have a single, focused message? Is his message simply a paean to the self, an autohagiography? Much of it is, yes. He is a modern-day Stagger Lee, an iconic swaggerer, a kind of twenty-first century street-smart, clever, charismatic antihero (and sometime criminal) whom polite society loves to celebrate. There might not be much else in Slikk's message beyond the continuation of his own myth of self, a rambling modern day picaresque of drugs, whores, and petty crime. With just one little exception: his ruthless satirization of the church, one of Slikk's perennial targets.

---

[15]Though it would be totally fair to accuse his "message" or his "focus" of being conservative in the sense that his portrayed persona-self is often that of a sexual god presiding over coteries of willing young women, priestess-like, who worship at the Slikkian altar.

This might seem, at first, to be but a minor theme in his work, but it is no accident that some of Slikk's very best music—and most thematically coherent albums—are heavily invested in Christian themes. Superficially, Slikk's treatment of the gospel is offensive, geared to shock religious mores and repulse believers. Going a little bit deeper, however, there is far too much of an investment in the gospel purely to make trouble.

Beyond basic religious blasphemy, Slikk's invocations of Christ are fairly lighthearted, almost celebratory of the religious subject matter, if one is allowed to imagine Christ as a charismatic figure and a flesh-and-blood man, rather than simply a vessel full to the brim with the Divinity. So much of Slikk's oeuvre toys with Christian themes that it almost, in toto, amounts to a apocryphal gospel all its own: Jesus Christ as a pimp among acolytes, followers, and doting prostitutes.

In *Sperm of Christ*, and in the mixtape *Jesus Boys* (with Mike Dece as the short-lived duo Proper Boys), the callouts, the spoken word sections, the paraphrasing of psalters, and the positioning of religious tenets at the forefront of the development of an alternative definition of the glory of Christ, there is a fairly deliberate and steady worldbuilding going on. It may be at odds with scripture only in the proper, textual sense—but less so among the apocryphal gospels where mythic and lurid tales of Christ abound. There are so many interpretations, translations, mistranslations, bastardizations, and mistransliterations of the Gospels that simply as another interpretation of the New Testament, one could identify, in toto, an Apocryphal Slikkian Gospel: the Gospel of Slikk and Christmobb.

Beyond this, there is such a rich tradition of riffing, so to speak, off of the basic stories of Christianity that if one were to object to calling the Slikkian verses a full-on gospel, these rhymes may still constitute the scripture of a Christian sect, or a cult. Cults of course need not satisfy mainstream Christianity at all—in fact, they are usually explicitly branded as antichristian, even if they claim to be Christian. Many groups that draw from the basic stories of the bible—say, for instance, Mormonism, Fundamentalist Mormonism, the Branch Davidian, Kabbalah—do the same thing: draw from biblical stories, question one or another aspect of those stories, and from inspired speculation build an alternative, sometimes wildly convincing or enthralling, narrative. In Mormonism, to use the most obvious example, Joseph Smith recast the story of the lost tribes of Israel to build the New World into the biblical mythos: he claimed that one of the lost tribes of Israel made its way to America and was cursed, branded with the mark of Cain, and became the New World's natives.

To cast Christ as a charismatic cult leader, with all the trappings—as we understand them now—of cult leaders is a reasonable lens of interpretation. If it is well known today that charismatic cult leaders—Warren Jeffs, Jim Jones, David Koresh—typically are megalomaniacal sociopaths, sexual predators, and manipulators, then we can assume those of the past were as well. I'm not saying Jesus Christ was this, or that he was anything, really: he is mostly myth, now, even if he was ever a real live human being. But it is refreshing to consider that the founder of Christianity might not have been a great guy, or a moral guy, even by his own definitions (as they've been reported or recorded by others, and retroactively placed in His mouth). This is typical: most cult leaders, while fleecing and preying upon their adherents, typically also profess and insist upon rigid adherence to a strict moral code and austere, devout asceticism. And the cycle of hypocrisy continues…

Yes—maybe a morally fraught Christ, a Christ who has a whole coterie of whores and willing cronies, who is known far and wide more for his large cock and his insatiable desire to simply live, love, and *fuck hoes*, is a more realistic Christ.

Is it artistic to challenge the status quo in these ways? To challenge decorum, to push boundaries? It might be that, in America, where nonindigenous artistic traditions have been imported piecemeal from elsewhere, and have been bound up in our uniquely frought system of capitalism for centuries, we don't actually have a way of understanding transgressive art outside of capitalism, which is to say, outside of the duality of greed and envy.[16] Greed drives the attention-seeking kind of transgressive art, one that shocks for the sake of publicity. Envy drives a reactionary kind of transgressive art, that which rails against artists, institutions, or traditions which have spurned the individual's work. Transgressive art aside, American culture—which is to say, again, capitalism, the specifically American flavor—has deeply degraded the idea of art—if ever there was any kind of cohesive, or coherent concept of capital-A 'Art' in America.

The progressive degradation of art in this country is (and was) inevitable, insofar as art has always been attached to commerce; that art is inextricable from its existence as a commodity, that its worth can be and often is measured in dollars.

---

[16]Capitalism itself, especially as it informs culture, is also reducible to the interplay between the dual sins of greed and envy.

One byproduct of this degradation is the idea that total comprehension of a created object is a virtue: the faster one can fully comprehend, thus fully consume, a work of art, the better it functions as a commodity. Individuals have been empowered to believe that a lack of quick comprehension equates to a failure on the artist's part to create something meaningful, valuable, *relatable*.

Ah, yes.

Genius, Novelty, Addiction, and the Average

At one point, either in our own lives or in history, we were told that it was valuable to engage with things and ideas that were not immediately understood, were not immediately "relatable"; that such engagement was good cognitive work; was *enriching*. Failing to understand something beyond our own purview was *bad*—it revealed one's provincialism, parochialism, narrow-mindedness. And this narrow-mindedness, down the road, could lead to worse things, like fascism—if not political fascism, then certainly cultural fascism, where works of art that are not understood are castigated as inferior by those who are too closed-minded to allow for a longer, slower arc of comprehension to play out.

I would posit that all works of art can be understood, but at different rates. To go even further, I think it's reasonable that an art object's comprehension rate—the length of time it takes a person to understand an art-object—exists in direct correlation to that art-object's merit. Meaning: something that can be instantaneously comprehended is quite possibly *not* art at all, and something that takes years of study, repeated viewings, listens, reads, etc.—even a whole lifetime of engagement—might be *a masterpiece.* This is not, of course, an original notion. Great works of art are magnetic, and draw a viewer/reader/listener back *ad infinitum*; they maintain and sustain their magic. If the act of viewing a painting, listening to an album, or reading a novel is an act of *consumption*, as capitalism would have it, then those paintings/albums/novels that *resist* their own consumption—that cannot be consumed and digested in one go, that continue to yield secrets on subsequent review—are true works of art.

Of course, the "better" art is, the longer it is likely to take an individual to gather the knowledge, or experience, required to understand it. As capitalism makes impatient little twits of all of us, we must resist the impulse to disregard, dismiss, or reject works of art which defy immediate assessment. Even those of us who profess to love the unusual stuff, those of us who have paid our dues in a subculture—one which has done a decent job of inculcating in us a deeper appreciation for the incomprehensible—ought to take care to watch our impulses regarding the unfamiliar.

Most people don't think about this; it's normal. Most people don't think about art. You could halve that statement: *most people don't think*. But, for those of us who enjoy thinking and who take pride in the labor of discovering better art, this kind of thinking is important. The ecstasy that comes from discovering the seemingly undiscoverable—we don't even know, we *cannot even fathom* what it is we're looking for—is powerful indeed, and keeps us going.

This feeling cannot be sold. One could argue, even, that this feeling can't be transmitted at all. When it seems to be—for instance, when one critic's near-religious experience of an artwork seems to be replicated in another—I wonder if that isn't a case of affectation: that the second critic has come to that artwork *hoping* to feel the same way, and in a sense has been *instructed* by the previous critique in how they might replicate the ecstatic experience. Less-than-ideally, such a scenario would be just another case of bandwagonning: everyone, every critic and blurber, every cultural talking head celebrating the same successful thing so that it continues to sell, continues to make *everyone* happy and make *everyone* more money, and the wheels spin, spin, spin…

But there must be exceptions: truly, broadly relatable works of art. In the best case, these would become our 'classics,' would populate our canons. The reality is that such universally appreciated works are more often outliers. Most popular things cannot, by the nature of their own popularity, be *particularly* interesting. *Particularness* is the opposite of *popularness*; to be *popular* is to appeal to the many: broadly, simply, easily; and, to that end, to have many *average* qualities—and *average* art isn't art. This is why a bestselling pop record—to take one example—does not necessarily indicate how an artist will fare years later. Aside from some statistical immortality, or some vague name recognition, they won't necessarily have the staying power of something that sold less well, but was truly extraordinary—something that needed time, maybe even a lot of time, for full comprehension and digestion.

By these criteria, it could be that the very best music in the universe *can't* be popular, so the probability of discovering the very best music—the work of, dare I say it, true geniuses and innovators—is slim. One *must* work for it, dig for it, *seek it out*, or else, passively, it will never be found, because capitalism doesn't work for this kind of art—the genius and the new—and doesn't know what to do with it, anyway; such systems can't understand it, because its understanding of all things begins and ends with profit, and *the average*, where profit is concerned, will always be king.

Consider another kind of extreme. If you're like me, a lot of people liking something can make that thing suspect. Of course there are exceptions, but for the most part, capitalism and art are at odds with one another. Commercial art—which is to say, advertising—is the nominal compromise in this dichotomy, but mostly things which strive for and achieve rarified heights of artistry *cannot also* be popular. The underground artist who suddenly strikes it rich is suspect—perhaps they have changed their formula; perhaps they have 'sold out.' I find it hard to care when the struggling artist is suddenly singing about a life of luxury and excess. Capitalism wants this—it helps the system self-replicate, like a virus, and sells the myth of the American/Capitalist dream—but I don't. Superwealth is a plague on society, as a whole, and an acute illness to the rich themselves—an addiction.

Likewise, an underground or indie artist who draws cachet for being under-the-radar but who creates art that is indistinguishable from the commercially-viable

is, if anything, equally as bad as a commercially successful pop artist—he is a dilettante, a poseur; inauthentic,
someone who is trying to gain access to "the industry"
while posing as an outsider to maintain his artistic credibility. It takes work, but it also takes guts, to choose to
make art, to choose to do something different, to do
something people have not seen or heard yet, or made
money off of—something, in short, that people won't
immediately know how to understand. That part takes
time, sometimes a lot. Paying attention to art is work,
and most people can't be bothered to do it.

No big deal.

Those of us who know how good *good art* can be,
how good it can feel to find something *amazing*, are
willing to do the work to find it. We don't want to be
mere consumers; not especially when the faceless, soul-
less structures of capitalism all around us would wish
that the sacred thing we love—*art*—could be totally
obliterated or else subsumed inside a commercial struc-
ture. If they could just find a way to *sell* us that thing

which we love so dearly, to have us consume it all at once, and thus to have to consume it all over again, driving profits… We will always resist this. Art will be that idleness, that twiddling of fingers, that pondering before a painting; the endless turning back of the needle to replay a song, over and over, to unravel its complexities; the slow, slaking read of a novel, once every five years, to rediscover who you were, then, as well as who you are, now, in light of every subsequent layer of revelation. Taking pleasure in art need unequivocally be a "waste" of time, a nonprofit venture, for that is its value.

Conclusion: Libertinism, Outsider Art, and Autodidacticism

In moving towards a conclusion, I wanted to address whether or not Ruben Slikk is a kind of outsider artist. Often this moniker implies that the artist is in some way an autodidact—which in the past might be a kind of excuse for a so-called primitive style, an outlier to the grand narrative of creative history. Today, however, I think this must mean something else, as one can achieve much more in self-learning now than even just a few years ago. To go a step further, an autodidactic approach might still be one of the few ways an artist can achieve something unique or original. Artistic 'training,' despite what it may have been in the past, is as much a process of indoctrination and the inculcating of rules as it is a drawing-out of one's full creative capabilities. The rules, of course, being those rules derived from the market, and artistic training taking the form of step-by-step instruction on how to make what's selling with just the barest minimum of originality to avoid getting sued.

"Autodidacticism" means something different now than it used to. It is not merely self-instruction, which, to some degree, every artist engages in. In the past, autodidacticism might simply have meant that an artist lived in the countryside, and never ventured into a city like Paris or London to explore the rich center of artistic culture, such that that culture might be reflected back in her own work. Showing, museum-going, and formal enrollment in art academies were all part of the engagement with official institutions of art, and if a provincial artist never did any of those things, and simply plied their artmaking alone in some village for years and years, she very likely might develop her methods as though organically. Autodidacticism in that sense is today almost impossible. From the internet artists will inevitably glean some knowledge of formal institutions of art, the *longue durée* of art history, standards of official art, the different schools and modes of art, and so on. A singular exception might be an artist who, because of unusual circumstances of poverty or upbringing, lacks access as a young person and then is summarily rejected from institutions later on, such that she is forced to continue her art on her own and in a sense in defiance of institutions which have shunned her praxis. Rejection alone might not constitute a condition of autodidacticism, though—every true artist experiences at least some rejection. But however possible or theoretical it might be that an older concept of autodidacticism can still exist today, it remains extremely unlikely.

Ruben Slikk is both autodidact and not. Having grown up in a rich music scene—southern Florida in the early 2000s has produced a lot of breakout rappers and hip-hop recording artists—he would have had access to a lot of underground music as well as what was popular at the time. In an interview with *6FT*, Slikk mentions a number of popular music groups—Dr. Dre, Snoop [Dogg], Bone Thugs N Harmony, EMINEM, but also Limp Bizkit, Marilyn Manson, Blink 182, System of a Down, The Offspring, as Slikk puts it, "real sloppy, sweaty…white boy shit"[17]—and so it's clear he was exposed to plenty of popular culture as well as whatever music was happening closer to home.

Is the transgressive in his art a conscious act, or is he just trying to shock and titillate? Is his brand of transgression simply motivated by greed? In the same interview with 6FT, Slikk says, at one point, "but you know, it's just music, 'cos, you know, we just want some money. Yeah. Yeah, I'm a greedy bastard. I just want some bread." When the interviewer asks whether or not "the bread was coming in when [Slikk] first started," Slikk responds that "naw…It was actually go-

---

[17]https://www.youtube.com/watch?v=VWRsqIQwIMc&t=186s

ing out."[18] So there might be a disconnect between the desire, which is a commercial one—simply to get paid for creative work—and the execution, which seems true to a creative vision at odds with existing commercial structures. Maybe his rap is simply too fresh for the mainstream, which is to say too transgressive, to ruthlessly *real*.

Hmm.

One wonders with how much of this analysis Slikk would actually agree. Thankfully what matters in the end is the artifact, and less the creators' intentions during its production. The life of a work of art, so long as it coincides with the artist's own life, is uneasy. People have needs beyond creative fulfillment, and often it is much easier to simply talk about art made by dead people, long ago. But we must also reckon with our own times, our own contemporaries, and contend with

---

[18]Ibid. A moment later the interviewer asks: "Damn, so, like, what were the biggest expenses and stuff?" And Slikk replies, "Damn. Everything. Oxygen. Oxygen was a top expense. You know. It was [the] top, most expensive item."

that messiness. The human being who exists alongside the art, if the art is really good, will always pose something of a disappointment by comparison. Also—to get back to Slikk—it seems that, despite a couple of lengthy public interviews, Slikk tends to speak very little about his intentions, politics, and outlook. He repeatedly stresses just how important money is—that it's the most important thing ever—but when asked about making music and making money, Slikk qualifies to the interviewer that "but if you love it [money] too much, it can be very dangerous," but that it's "safer to get it than to not."[19] He is asked about his art repeatedly, but his answers are often simple, deliberately shutting down any deep diving. Unlike with others whose big mouths preclude possible generous interpretations of their work, Slikk is mostly a cipher, and therefore his work remains open to interpretation.

Along with interpretation, how much does morality matter? Must art be moral? Can art be amoral? A friend

---

[19]At approximately 7:58-8:12.

of mine once told me there's no such thing as music that is bad for you. Must we separate art from its maker in order to properly interpret it, as practitioners of New Criticism prefer? Slikk's work, set apart from a controversial personage? Sade's novels and his libertine philosophy, independent of the man? And, to consider de Sade, which part was less moral: the work or the man? The unfair nature of his hereditary nobility? The indulgent wealth that presupposed his plunge into excesses of sexual debauchery and lurid innovation, and the ways in which his pursuit of sexual extremes eventually infringed upon the humanity of others?

Trying to parse the moral differences between an historical figure and the literature he produced might be a chicken-and-egg kind of question, but I would suggest that the economic inequalities are the greatest sin, the sin which begat the others. To take a more recent example—in considering the art apart from the criminal personage who created it—R Kelly's art is bad art because it is amoral in addition to being commercial; and because, as a friend of mine said: "he cares too much." The art becomes almost a kind of accessory to the crimes, and the self-persona in the artwork a kind of accomplice to the criminal act. Let's hope Slikk doesn't find a similar path—that the art can remain by degrees a dispassionate compulsion apart from any other compulsions he might have, libertine compulsions, the kind which draw the ire of society's moral guardians.

Notes

For a good example of a transgressive novel, see Bataille, Georges and Dovid Bergelson, trans. *Story of the Eye*. City Lights Press: 2001. This is a classic. While we don't talk about literature too much, this and the *120 Days of Sodom* by the Marquis de Sade are probably the two most world famous transgressive novels of all time. And both by French guys. For an understanding of envy as a driver of capitalism, see Girard, René and Haven, Cynthia L., ed. *Conversations with René Girard: Prophet of Envy*. Bloomsbury Press: 2020. Johann Wolfgang von Goethe's *Venetian Epigrams* can be found online in different places. For an introduction to Goethe as a rabblerouser and incorrigible rake—his transgressive side—see "Super Goethe" by Ferdinand Mount in the *New York Review of Books* (December 21, 2017), a review article of *Goethe: Life as a Work of Art* by

Rüdiger Safranski, translated from the German by David Dollenmayer. Liveright, 2017. For maybe the best example of a transgressive Frank Zappa album, see *The Man From Utopia* (Barking Pumpkin, 1983). For an overview of the politics of that man, see the most recent (2020) documentary *Zappa* by Alex Winter. (Magnolia Pictures), prod. Jim Reeve, Robert Halmi). There were only two extensive interviews with Ruben Slikk available at the writing of this book, both available on YouTube. The first is with 6FT (2017): https://www.youtube.com/watch?v=VWRsqIQwIMc &t=186s and the second with The Mars Files (2016): https://www.youtube.com/watch?v=2_WpldZc-Rs.

Appendix

(Woefully Incomplete) Ruben Slikk Discography

As Ruben Slikk via the Archive

ASTRO TRAVEL

BIBLEBOYZ *the scriptures of cum*

BITCHBOSS WARRIORZ

BIXMIXX WHODDIE

CANDYFLOSS

CHALKZONE

DIARIES OF A KOKEBOSS HLORD

FUCKNIGGAFUNERAL

HELL MONEY

HOTSEXXXX

IGLESIA DE FISHMIXXMAS CHRISTO

KIKI FREAK ME KUMFUCKLANTHROPY

KING ASTROSLIKK THE MAGNIFICENT

KODEEN MUTANTZ

LAUNDERBO$$

NEW WORLD MURDA

PO$HKRAKK

POSHGANG IZ AN ARMY

RAPGAMERAPEMOBB

SPERM OF CHRIST

THEORYBOYZ

The night b4 beexmas Kokane Vatican of jeez

WHORELORD BANKBOSS FETISH SLIKK x DANKGOD

YOUNG FOOD : HEROINE CHRIST;.1-

YUNGFISHMIXXX : LIVIN LIFE SO PLUSH

<u>**As PROPR BOYZ**</u> **(w/Mike Dece)**
JESUS BOYZ (mixtape)

<u>**With METRO ZU**</u>
A[i]R
BEACHRUNNER
Buddha Therapy
COKEYSHORESMOTORSPORTS VOL. 1
COKEYSHORESMOTORSPORTS VOL. 3
ELISE
HAITIAN SILK
HEAVEN
ICE CREAM WORLD
KUSHPAK 3 VOL. 1, KUSHPAK 3 VOL. 2, KUSHPAK 3 VOL. 3, KUSKPAK 3 VOL. 4, KUSHPAK 3 VOL. 5, KUSHPAK 3 VOL. 6, KUSH-PAK 3 VOL. 7, KUSHPAK 3 VOL. 8, KUSHPAK 3 VOL. 9, KUSHPAK 3 VOL. 10
LIQUIT DINOSAUR
Mink Rug
POSH PHARAOH
REBEL FLEET 3
SEX SHOOTER
SHROOMTARD 6
SYMBOLIC 2
TIME CRYSTAL
TIME CRYSTAL 2
Z UNIT
ZUOLOGY

Other Albums and Associated Projects

TURD FIGHTER
DAT SHIT 4 CUMSTUFFINGTON
GOONY TOONZ (w/DJ Smokey)
FUKKIN ON DEEZ HOES (feat Lofty305 & Agoff)
YELLOW BRICK ROAD EP
SLIKKFREE
HMOBBB (mixtape*)*
CHRISTMOBB the Mixtape (mixtape*)*
HOTSEXXXX
YUNG ZEUS (w/ZChronik*)*
YUNG ZEUS 2 (w/ZChronik*)*
666 SHIT (w/DJ Smokey*)*
NIGHT OF THE LIVING CUMCHRIST (Bozo Da Wam feat Ruben Slikk)
ZANLORD KULT MOB
CHRIST RAPE : ABUNDANCE MOBB
CLEVER MONEY GANG (Kirb la Goop & Avi Twat feat. Ruben Slikk*)*
LDRBMFK (Kirb la Goop feat. Ruben Slikk*)*
KRUNCHY BRIZZLE: LEANED AND SAMU-RAIED VOL. 2 (w/?*)*
DENZEL CURRY: KING OF THE MISCHIEVOUS SOUTH VOLUME 1 UNDERGROUND TAPE 1996 (w/Ruben Slikk)
HONOR AND MAJESTY (Bozo da Wam feat Slikk)
NIGHT OF THE LIVING CUM CHRIST (")
Strange Love (")

Notable Songs and Singles

"Bad Bitch Whoddie"
"Fuck My Cum"
"Girls Gone Wild"
"Like a Niggr"
"Assistant Pimpin"
"Myself" (lanyard)
"Jizz4Life"
"N— of the Year"
"POLYGAMIST"
"Tears on my Cock"
"Catch me with that Sack"
"DaffyDuckCryin"
"Golds on my Weiner"
"Be Yo Guh"
"Show Dat Krakk"
"Sukk my Fukk"
"Koko Agua"
"I Rob 2 Much"
"Boonjie"
"Eggnoggio Challenge"
"STR8THEXX"
"I Feel Great" (ZChronic feat Slikk)
"N— Gotta Have It"
"Ho Money" (w/Lofty 305 & Mr. B)

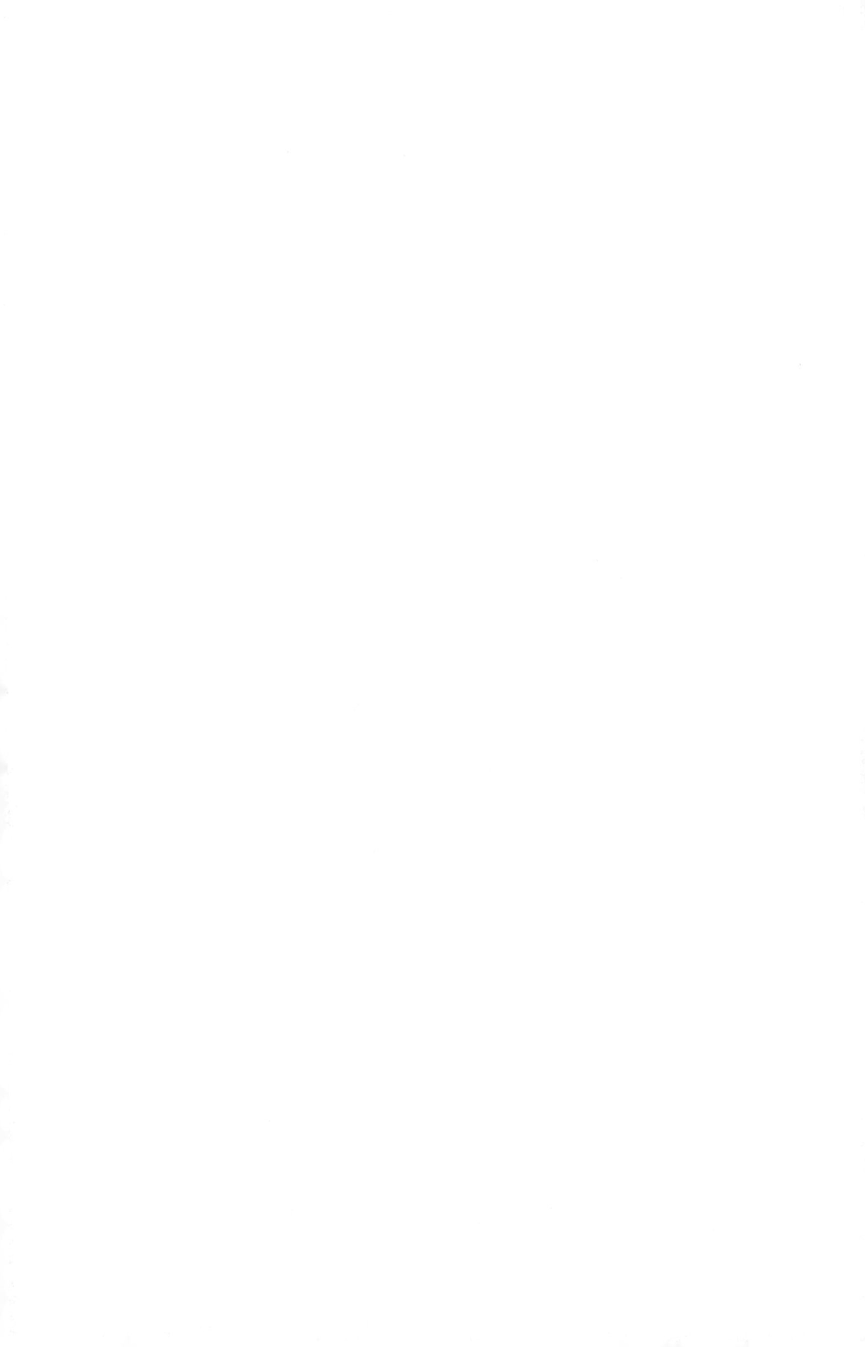

DYNAMO VERLAG BOOKS

Telescopes and Other People
JOSH NORMAN

Daughters of Monsters
MELISSA GOODRICH

Peregrine Nation
LUCIAN MATTISON

The Much Love Sad Dawg Trio
MATTHEW SADLER

Driving Around, Looking in Other People's Windows
CL BLEDSOE

Star Things
JESS L PARKER

On Ruben Slikk
CALEB TRUE

Local Weather
ANDREW SQUITIRO

A Human Moon
ALLELIAH NUGUID

DYNAMOVERLAG.COM